L-4.3
P-0.5

W9-ASM-187

EDGE
BOOKS

X-SPORTS

AGGRESSIVE IN-LINE SKATING

BY ANN WEIL

CONSULTANT:
KALINDA MATHIS
EXECUTIVE DIRECTOR
INTERNATIONAL INLINE
SKATING ASSOCIATION

Capstone
press

Mankato, Minnesota

Edge Books are published by Capstone Press
151 Good Counsel Drive, P.O. Box 669, Mankato, Minnesota 56002
www.capstonepress.com

Library of Congress Cataloging-in-Publication Data
Weil, Ann.
    Aggressive in-line skating / by Ann Weil.
    p. cm.—(Edge books. X-sports)
    Includes bibliographical references and index.
    Contents: Aggressive in-line skating—Gear—Tricks and extreme moves—
Famous pros—Glossary.
    ISBN 0-7368-2708-0 (hardcover)
    1. In-line skating—Juvenile literature. [1. In-line skating. 2. Extreme sports.]
I. Title. II. Series.
GV859.73.W45 2005
796.21—dc22   2003026088

Editorial Credits
James Anderson, editor; Jason Knudson, designer; Jo Miller, photo researcher;
    Eric Kudalis, product planning editor

Photo Credits
AP/WideWorld Photos/Chris Polk, 5
Corbis/Duomo, (cover), 9 (bottom), 11, 28; NewSport/Al Fuchs, 7, 13, 16, 21, 27;
    Richard Hamilton Smith, 9 (top)
Getty Images, Inc./Stanley Chou, 6, 15, 25
Mercury Press/Isaac Hernandez, 18; Marcelo Moreno, 19

1 2 3 4 5 6 09 08 07 06 05 04

TABLE OF CONTENTS

CHAPTER 1

AGGRESSIVE IN-LINE SKATING

Fabiola da Silva's first run at the 2003 Summer X Games was not her best. But her second run was terrific. She did a 540 spin, then a perfect forward 360. She finished with an alley-oop soul. Da Silva's performance won her the gold medal in the women's in-line park event.

The first in-line skaters did stunts on local streets and sidewalks. Many top skaters now compete in worldwide events. These skaters take part in the X Games, the Gravity Games, and other extreme sports competitions.

LEARN ABOUT:

- Fabiola da Silva
- The triple Lindy
- Halfpipes

Fabiola da Silva improved her skating at the 2003 X Games.

SKATING STYLES

Park skating is one style of in-line skating. Park events are held on skatepark courses. Park skaters do tricks on rails, benches, stairs, and other obstacles. Some park events are also called street events.

Street skaters do grinds during contests.

EDGE FACT

During some events, park skaters have 60 seconds to use as many obstacles as they can. Vert skaters have 45 seconds to complete their moves.

Vert is short for vertical. Vert events are held on halfpipe ramps. Skaters gain speed on the halfpipe's curves. They do tricks above the ramp.

Only the top athletes compete in the X Games and the Gravity Games. Some pros take part in both street and vert events. Others focus on just one style.

Pro in-line skaters show off new moves at contests. At the 2002 Gravity Games, Matt Lindy was the first in-line skater to do a triple backflip at an event. The move became known as the triple Lindy.

Matt Lindy celebrated after landing a triple backflip.

PARK SKATING

Like skateboarding, aggressive in-line skating began on streets and public parks. But many people did not like skaters jumping stairs, curbs, and benches in public places.

Many cities now have skateparks for in-line skaters. These parks have the same obstacles found on streets, on sidewalks, and in public parks.

VERT SKATING

Aggressive in-line skaters use skatepark ramps to do tricks they can't do on the ground. Halfpipes are the most popular ramp. These U-shaped ramps are usually made of wood. Small halfpipes are called miniramps. They are about 3 feet (1 meter) high. Some large halfpipes are more than 12 feet (3.7 meters) high.

Skaters build up speed as they ride the walls of a halfpipe. They fly high into the air. They do flips, grabs, and other moves above the ramp's coping.

Street skaters do moves on obstacles such as handrails.

Vert skaters do moves above a halfpipe ramp.

9

CHAPTER 2

AGGRESSIVE IN-LINE GEAR

Aggressive in-line skaters must have the right equipment. Skaters need good skates with the right size wheels. Helmets and other gear protect skaters when they fall.

SKATES

Skaters can choose from several kinds of in-line skates. Some skates are just for playing hockey. Some are for fitness skaters. Aggressive in-line skates are tougher than other skates. They can stand up to hard landings and grinds.

LEARN ABOUT:

- Grind plates
- Durometer
- Helmets

Aggressive in-line skaters have strong skates and equipment.

The skate's frame connects the boot to the wheels. Aggressive in-line skates used to have grind plates on the bottom of the frame. These small metal plates protected the skate during grinds. Now most skates have a Universal Frame System (UFS). Skaters can replace frames quickly and easily.

WHEELS

In-line skate wheels come in different sizes. Aggressive skaters use small wheels. There is more space between the wheels to do grinds.

A wheel's hardness is measured in durometers. Vert skaters need extra speed for their moves. They often use hard wheels with a high durometer. Street skaters also use hard wheels. Hard wheels do not wear as quickly from rough street moves.

EDGE FACT

Uneven wheels are not safe. To avoid uneven wear, active skaters should rotate their wheels about once each week.

HELMETS AND PADS

All skaters should wear helmets. In-line skating helmets are made of hard plastic materials. Foam padding inside the helmet protects the skater's head. Vert skaters should always wear helmets when they are on the halfpipe, even if it isn't their turn to skate.

Skaters also use pads to protect themselves. Skaters wear wrist guards, knee pads, and elbow pads.

Skaters wear helmets and pads.

CHAPTER 3

TRICKS AND EXTREME MOVES

Beginning skaters learn basic moves. They do curb grinds and easy grabs. Pro street skaters can do difficult street moves like 540s. Pro vert skaters do flips and spins on halfpipes. They sometimes do moves 10 feet (3 meters) above the ramp.

BEGINNING MOVES

One of the first moves most skaters learn is a grind. A grind is sliding on a rail, curb, or other obstacle. Skaters begin grinds by skating up to objects and jumping onto them. Skaters land between the middle wheels. They drag the skate's frame sideways over the object.

LEARN ABOUT:

- Soul grind
- Sad plant
- Double flat spin

Many skaters do different styles of grinds.

15

Skaters have different foot positions for grinds. They do frontside grinds with their bodies facing the obstacle. They grind on the outside edge of the skate. A backside grind is the same as a frontside, but the skater faces away from the obstacle.

16

Skaters also do other grinds. For a royale, skaters grind on the inside edge of the front skate and the outside edge of the back skate. For a soul grind, the back foot grinds on the sole of the skate.

Skaters can grind with both skates or just one. A backslide is a one-footed grind. Skaters grab the front foot while the back skate grinds on an object.

STALLS

Beginning skaters also do stalls. They jump onto a curb or rail, stop for a few seconds, and jump off. Skaters add stalls to other moves. For a rewind, skaters spin after doing a stall.

Skaters also do stalls with their hands. Skaters stall during hand plants. Street skaters do a handstand on an obstacle. Vert skaters do a handstand on the coping of a halfpipe. This trick is also called an invert. To do a sad plant, skaters do an invert using only one hand.

GRABS

Many skaters add grabs to moves. During a grab, skaters hold one or both skates. Grabs can be done with straight legs or with the legs bent or crossed.

Two basic grabs are the solo grab and the mono grab. For the solo grab, skaters move forward on one foot while grabbing the other foot. The mono grab is like a solo grab, but the skater moves backward.

Skaters show off new grab moves during competitions.

Skaters do stale grabs when they grab near the wheels of a skate.

Skaters also do more difficult grabs. During a stale grab, they grab near the wheels of a skate. During a stalefish grab, skaters reach behind with one hand to grab the outside of the opposite skate.

Some grabs are crossed. Skaters reach across with one hand to grab a skate on the other side. Skaters may cross their skates instead of reaching over. This move is a crossed-up grab.

SPINS

Street and vert skaters do spin moves. Street skaters do 360 spins off obstacles. A 360 spin is a full turn in the air. Some street skaters do 540s, or one and one-half turns in the air.

Vert skaters get higher in the air. They have more time to do spins before they land. They can get enough air to do a 720. A 720 is two full turns. Some skaters have done 1080s. They spin three times before landing on the ramp.

Spins are popular at contests. Pro skater Taig Khris did a double flatspin during the 2002 Gravity Games. His body faced the ramp while he spun twice in the air. He was the first skater to do this move in a contest.

EDGE FACT

Skating down steps is called stair bashing. Skaters go forward, backward, or sideways during this dangerous move.

Spins are popular moves at competitions.

FLIPS

Most skaters believe flips are more difficult than grinds, grabs, or spins. Flips are usually done on vert ramps. Skaters can flip forward during a frontflip or backward during a backflip.

Some skaters do double or even triple flips. Eito Yasutoko did a double backflip 180 and a double backflip to flat spin at the 2003 Gravity Games.

HOW TO DO A
FAKIE 360 SPIN

3. The skater lands skating backward, or fakie.

CHAPTER 4

FAMOUS PROS

The X Games and the Gravity Games are two of aggressive in-line skating's most popular events. Skaters around the world hope to take part in these contests.

TAKESHI AND EITO YASUTOKO

Takeshi and Eito Yasutoko are brothers. They grew up on skates. Their parents were roller disco dancers. Now their parents own a skatepark in Japan. Takeshi and Eito compete all over the world.

LEARN ABOUT:

- Yasutoko brothers
- The Fabiola rule
- 1080

Takeshi and Eito Yasutoko are both X Games winners.

Takeshi went pro at age 9. At 11, he went to the 1998 X Games. Takeshi is the youngest athlete to ever compete at the X Games. He is also the youngest in-line skater to win a medal. He won the silver medal in 2000 and the gold in 2002.

Eito won the vert gold medal at the 2003 Gravity Games. He was the first skater to do a 1080 flatspin in competition.

FABIOLA DA SILVA

Fabiola da Silva grew up in Sao Paulo, Brazil. Her dad gave her a pair of roller skates when she was 17 years old. Today, da Silva is the best-known female in-line skater. She won a gold medal at the 2003 X Games. It was her seventh gold medal. She has won more X Games medals than any other female athlete.

The Aggressive Skaters Association (ASA) introduced the "Fabiola Rule" in 2000. The rule allows female skaters to compete against male skaters. The rule was named after da Silva because she often competed against male skaters.

TAIG KHRIS

Taig Khris was born in Algeria. He has won gold medals for vert at the X Games and the Gravity Games. He did the first double flatspin at the 2002 Gravity Games.

Khris is one of the busiest in-line skaters. In six years, he competed in more than 100 events. Although he competes all over the world, he doesn't have trouble communicating. Khris speaks five languages.

Fabiola da Silva is sometimes the only female skater in contests.

Jaren Grob competes in vert and park events.

JAREN GROB

Jaren Grob was born in Orem, Utah, in 1981. In 1994, Grob started competing. He was 13 years old.

In less than 10 years, Grob was an X Games star. He won a gold medal in 2001 and 2002. He won a silver medal at the 2003 X Games. Grob is the only park event skater to win gold medals two years in a row.

AGGRESSIVE IN-LINE'S FUTURE

Aggressive in-line skaters all over the world invent new moves. Beginning skaters watch the X Games, the Gravity Games, and other contests on TV. They practice the moves. The skaters train and prepare for big events.

These skaters are aggressive in-line's future. They learn moves and take care of their bodies. They wear the right gear to protect them from injuries. Well-prepared skaters keep the sport exciting.

GLOSSARY

aggressive (uh-GREH-siv)—more forceful and intense than usual

communicate (kuh-MYOO-nuh-kate)—to share information, ideas, or feelings with another person by talking or writing

competition (kom-puh-TISH-uhn)—a contest between two or more people

coping (KO-ping)—the metal bar at the top edge of a halfpipe

durometer (da-RAH-muh-tor)—the measurement of an in-line skate wheel's hardness

obstacle (OB-stuh-kuhl)—an object in a skatepark; street skaters do moves off obstacles.

performance (pur-FOR-muhns)—the public presentation of a skater's moves

position (puh-ZISH-uhn)—the way a skater's feet are placed

vert (VURT)—a type of skating that involves halfpipe ramps; vert skaters do moves above the ramps.

READ MORE

Blomquist, Christopher. *In-line Skating at the X Games.* A Kid's Guide to the X Games. New York: PowerKids Press, 2003.

Glidewell, Steve. *Inline Skating.* Extreme Sports. Minneapolis: Lerner, 2004.

Miller, Chuck. *In-line Skating.* Extreme Sports. Austin, Texas: Steadwell Books, 2002.

INTERNET SITES

FactHound offers a safe, fun way to find Internet sites related to this book. All of the sites on FactHound have been researched by our staff.

Here's how:

1. Visit *www.facthound.com*
2. Type in this special code **0736827080** for age-appropriate sites. Or enter a search word related to this book for a more general search.
3. Click on the **Fetch It** button.

FactHound will fetch the best sites for you!

INDEX